The Black Regiment

OF THE AMERICAN REVOLUTION

The SIEGE OF RHODE ISLAND, taken from Mr Brindley's House, on the 25th of August, 1778.

This view of the Battle of Rhode Island appeared in a magazine of the period. (Library of Congress, Library of Congress Rare Books and Special Collections Division, LC-USZ62-16834)

LINDA CROTTA BRENNAN

ILLUSTRATED BY CHERYL KIRK NOLL

Thymely Press

The officers from Rhode Island were worried. Their soldiers had spent the bitter winter of 1777 with General George Washington's Continental Army, camped at Valley Forge, Pennsylvania. They were hungry and cold, dressed in rags, and living in huts. Now most of the men's enlistments were over, and many were going home.

Rhode Island was supposed to have two forces, the 1st and 2nd Regiments, but there were only 400 soldiers left. That was half the number they needed. General James Varnum, Colonel Christopher Greene, Captain Stephen Olney, and the other officers decided to combine the remaining men into the 2nd Regiment. But how would they raise enough men for a new 1st Regiment?

With the British occupying Newport, its biggest city, Rhode Island needed most of its men at home. More than a thousand Rhode Islanders were already fighting as sailors on naval ships and privateers. Many of the remaining men couldn't or wouldn't fight. Some were Quakers whose religion forbade fighting. Others were farmers or tradesman who were needed to provide food and goods so the state could survive.

By February only 50 men had volunteered. General Washington had ordered two Rhode Island regiments to report for duty. What could the officers do?

Then General Varnum had an idea. Why not enlist slaves? Rhode Island had more slaves than any other state in New England. Newport was a major slaving port before the war, and many slaves worked on plantations in the southern part of the state.

There were already a few black men in the 2nd Rhode Island Regiment, and the officers knew the worth of these soldiers. They backed Varnum's plan to raise a black regiment. Colonel Greene was chosen to lead it. Now they had to convince their state to try it.

FINDING MEN TO FIGHT

By law, men had to serve in their local militia. But there was no forced draft for Washington's Continental Army, because there was no strong central government to enact a draft. Instead, each state was required to send a certain number of regiments to fight in the Continental Army. If they didn't send those regiments, the states would be fined.

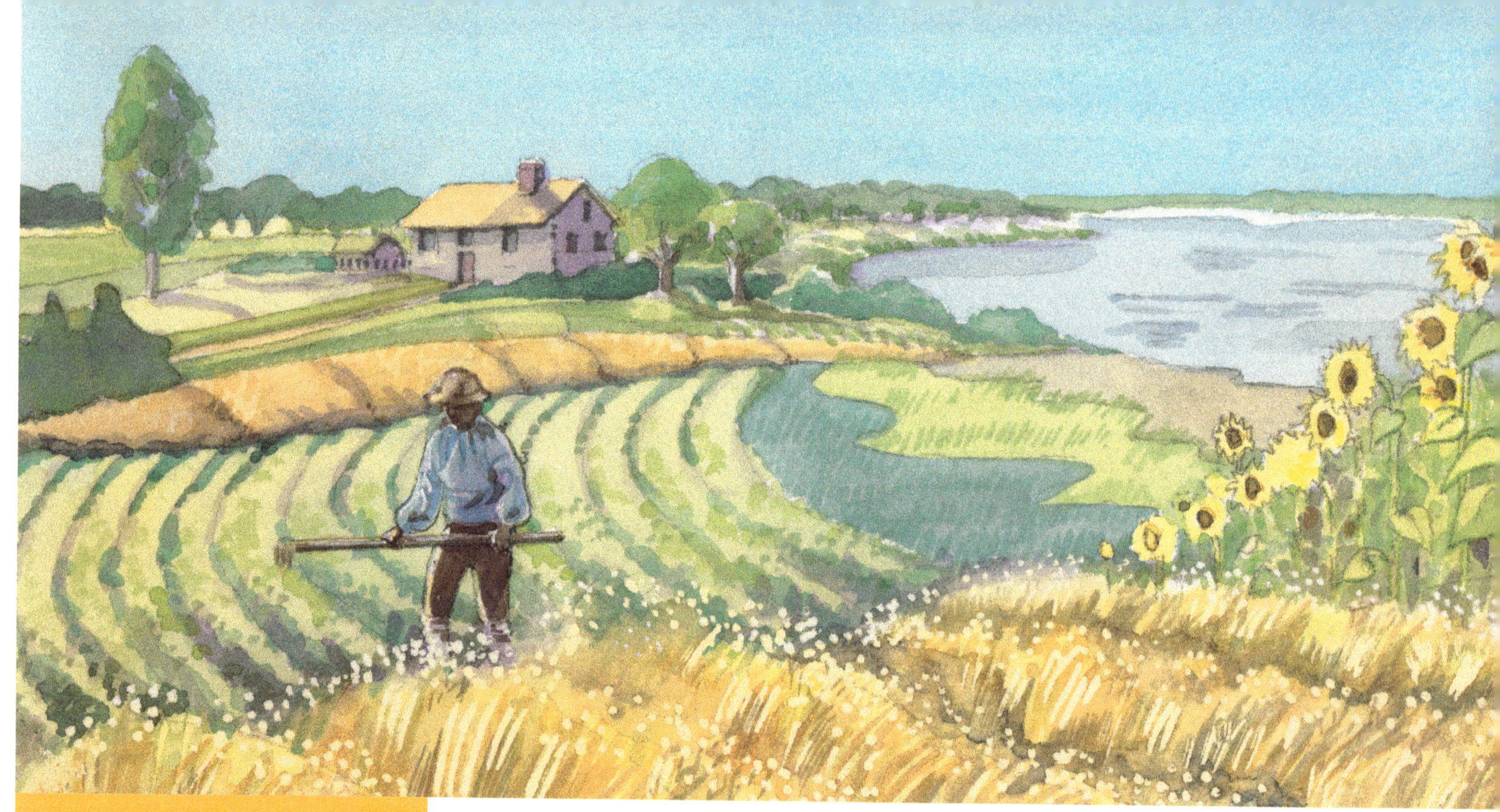

NATIVE AMERICAN SLAVES

King Philip's War was a long and bloody fight between the New England colonists and an alliance of Native American tribes. The colonists won the war in 1676, taking many Native Americans captive. These captives were sold into slavery. A hundred years later, at the time of the Revolutionary War, many Native Americans were still slaves.

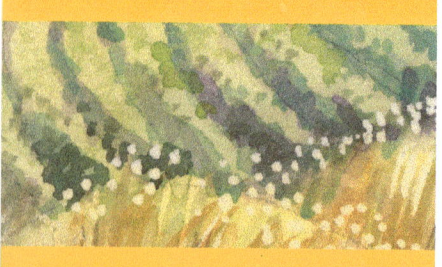

The plan for the Black Regiment was placed before the Rhode Island legislature. Many of the state's lawmakers and wealthiest citizens were slave traders and slave owners. They were against the idea of arming slaves. They worried that enlisting slaves in the army would brew trouble with the slaves left behind. But no one had any better ideas for finding the soldiers Rhode Island needed.

So on February 23, 1778, the Rhode Island legislature passed the historic act creating a new 1st Rhode Island Regiment. The law stated that "every able-bodied Negro, mulatto, or Indian man-slave" could enlist. Rhode Island would pay owners for their slaves.

Slaves had fought alongside white men in America before, but they never had the same pay or privileges. The new Rhode Island law said that slaves who enlisted would be given the same "bounty and wages" as white soldiers. More importantly, it said that "upon passing muster by Colonel Christopher Greene," each slave would be free.

Many owners tried to talk their slaves out of joining. But slaves jumped at the chance for freedom. After four months, Rhode Island stopped the program. Too many slave owners complained, and paying for slaves was too expensive. But by then there were close to 200 men in the 1st Rhode

Island Regiment, which later became known as the Black Regiment. Most of the enlistees were black men, but some were white.

Who were the "blacks" in the Black Regiment? Although a few of them were free blacks, like Richard Cozzens, most of them were slaves. Some, like Prince Jenks, were Africans who had been captured from their native countries and carried across the sea into slavery. Some, like Joseph Brown, were African-Americans whose parents or grandparents had been born in Africa. Still others, like Harry Gideon, were Native American slaves. Many were of mixed race, with African, Native American, and European blood. These people of mixed blood were sometimes called "mulattoes."

Most, like Caesar Updike and Cuff Gardner, were farm slaves from plantations in southern Rhode Island. Some came from cities, like Jack Champlin from Newport. Many were laborers, like Henry Tabor, but some had special skills, like Cato Varnum, a carpenter. Most were in their teens or early twenties, but Asher Polock was 52 and Pharoh Hazard was 53.

Whether they came from the country or the city, were laborers or skilled workers, young or old, Native American or African American, these men all had a very special reason for joining the Black Regiment. They were fighting not just for their country's freedom; they were fighting for their own freedom.

Black men served as sailors aboard privateers and in the Continental Navy during the Revolutionary War.

1. HALF-COCK FIRELOCK
2. HANDLE CARTRIDGE
3. PRIME
4. SHUT PAN
5. CHARGE WITH CARTRIDGE
6. DRAW RAMMER
7. RAM DOWN CARTRIDGE
8. RETURN RAMMER
9. SHOULDER FIRELOCK
10. POISE FIRELOCK
11. FULL-COCK FIRELOCK
12. TAKE AIM
13. FIRE **!**

GENERAL VON STEUBEN'S MANUAL EXERCISE: LOADING AND FIRING

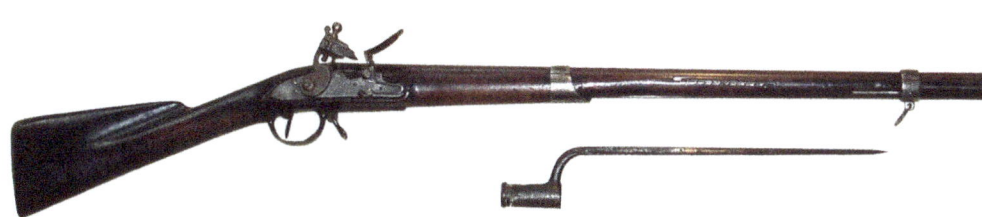

(Musket image courtesy of Kirk Hindman)

Although some free blacks served as soldiers in largely white regiments, black slaves usually were used as servants in the Continental Army. They worked as cooks or waiters or were sent out to forage for food. But the men of the 1st Rhode Island Regiment were soldiers.

Their commander, Colonel Greene, led the Black Regiment in endless drills. The men marched in formation. They learned the complicated steps of firing a musket. They learned to fire those muskets in unison. They practiced over and over until they could act by instinct even during the confusion of a battle. But the Black Regiment didn't have long to prepare before they were called to war.

MUSKETRY

The muskets used in the Revolutionary War were not very accurate. Since any one musket ball was unlikely to hit its target, soldiers were trained to fire in unison. That way at least some of the balls might hit their mark. Firing a musket was complicated, and soldiers practiced the steps every day until they could perform them quickly and smoothly.

GUNS AND BAYONETS

During a battle, blocks of soldiers marched together. When they got within range of the enemy, they fired their muskets in unison. Then they had to reload. Trained soldiers could load and fire four times a minute. This was too slow when soldiers were face-to-face with an enemy, so at close range, they fought with bayonets. These were blades fixed to the end of their muskets. Many American soldiers didn't have bayonets. Some of the Black Regiment had them, but some did not.

The British occupied Newport, Rhode Island, on the southern tip of an island in Narragansett Bay. From Newport, the British could block shipping and trade to the rest of the state. This was crippling to Rhode Island because, at that time, travel by water was easier than travel by land.

The Americans had tried to force the British out of Newport twice before and failed. Now America's allies, the French, promised to help. George Washington put General John Sullivan in charge of the Battle of Rhode Island. In the summer of 1778, Sullivan called for troops to gather at Fort

The map illustration contains the following labels:

QUEBEC (CANADA)

NORTH

MONTREAL

MASSACHUSETTS (MAINE)

THE HAMPSHIRE GRANTS (VERMONT)

NEW HAMPSHIRE

PORTSMOUTH

ALBANY

BOSTON

NEW YORK

MASSACHUSETTS

HARTFORD

RHODE ISLAND

NEWPORT

CONNECTICUT

NEW YORK CITY

ATLANTIC OCEAN

NEW JERSEY

Newport, Rhode Island, was strategically important to the British. It was one of the best harbors and largest ports in the colonies. It was close to Boston, and a fleet stationed there could control shipping bound for Connecticut and New York. (As shown on the map, some political borders were not well defined at this time.)

Barton, on the mainland north of Newport. Over 10,000 men answered the call. Militia streamed in from all over Rhode Island and the other New England states. Most of the militiamen were farmers who left their fields in the middle of harvest. They were called up for one month's service as soldiers, to fight this particular battle. General Sullivan described the militiamen as a "motley and disarranged Chaos" that he had to whip into order. The newly formed Black Regiment joined the other regiments and militias gathering at Fort Barton.

On July 29, a fleet of twelve French ships sailed into Narragansett Bay with Count D'Estaing in command. He was a land soldier, not used to naval battles, and his naval officers didn't trust him. But he brought 4,000 French soldiers on board his ships. And he had firepower desperately needed by the Americans.

General Sullivan boarded the mighty French flagship, studded with ninety guns. D'Estaing greeted Sullivan with flowery French courtesy. Sullivan responded with New England coolness. D'Estaing expected the Americans to provide supplies for his men, thirsty and suffering from scurvy after five months at sea. Sullivan had few supplies to offer him.

Still the two men worked together to create a carefully coordinated plan to drive the British from Newport. The French ships would fight their way up the bay west of Newport on August 8. On the night of the ninth, American troops at Fort Barton would use small boats to ferry over to Newport's island. On the eleventh, the Americans would sweep down from the north to attack the British while the French attacked from the west.

Meanwhile the British scurried to prepare defenses. Because they were outgunned, the British sank their own ships in the harbor to prevent the French ships from coming too close. They cut down trees to block the roads into Newport. They cleared woods and burned houses so they would have a clear view of attacking troops. Then they pulled all their soldiers back to strong positions just north of the city to defend it.

The storm-battered French fleet leaves Rhode Island just before the planned attack on Newport. Count D'Estaing's flagship appears to the left of center. It had lost all its masts in the storm, and its shortened rig is a temporary repair. Note some of its masts in the water, under tow. (Library of Congress)

General Sullivan discovered that the British had abandoned the north end of the island. So on the night of August 8, he ferried his troops over from Fort Barton, a day ahead of schedule. Men like Peter Hazzard, Jehue Pomp, Cuff Roberts, and the others in the Black Regiment had been soldiers for a only few months. This would be their first fight. They had much to think about as they were rowed across the bay, the waves slapping against their boats in the moonlight.

Unfortunately, General Sullivan hadn't told the French about his change of plan. D'Estaing was upset that the strategy for a coordinated attack was ruined. The French commander landed to discuss matters with Sullivan. As the morning mist burned off, he saw thirty-six British ships sail into the harbor. D'Estaing ordered his ships to prepare for battle.

General Sullivan asked D'Estaing to leave some of his French soldiers on shore to help the Americans with the land fight. D'Estaing refused. Then the French sailed out to meet the British fleet.

For two days the French and British warships maneuvered. They elbowed each other for the best wind position for battle. Then a hurricane blew in. It raged for three full days. Wild winds scattered the fleet. Mighty waves hammered the ships. D'Estaing's flagship lost all her masts and her rudder. Finding her disabled, the British attacked. Though she was rescued by some of her sister ships, D'Estaing's ship suffered severe casualties and damage. So did many other ships in the British and French fleets.

The hurricane battered the troops on land, too. Sullivan described it in a letter to Washington as "a storm so violent That it Last Night Blew Down & Tore & almost Ruined all the Tents I had. … My men are mostly Lying under fences half Covered with water without Ammunition & with Arms rendered useless."

Sullivan anxiously awaited D'Estaing's return. In the meantime, he marched his troops south, into positions opposite the British. For five days the armies exchanged heated cannon fire.

Finally D'Estaing limped back. He announced that his fleet would sail to Boston for repairs. General Sullivan begged him to stay just one more day, but D'Estaing refused. His first duty was the safety of his fleet. If repairs could be completed quickly, he would return.

Sullivan and many of his troops resented the French leaving. One American soldier wrote, "The French fleet left us today bound to Boston and I think left us in the most rascally manner."

According to an American general, the departure of the French "struck such a panic among the militia and volunteers that they began to desert in shoals." Most of the militiamen were farmers and craftsmen who had signed up to fight just this one battle. At about the same time, the governor of Rhode Island called his militia home to guard the mainland. Between desertions and the recall of the Rhode Island militia, Sullivan lost 3,000 men. But the men of the Black Regiment, men like Jack Champlin and Henry Tabor, were fighting for their own freedom. They were committed to fight for the length of the war. The Black Regiment stayed.

Sullivan got word that the British general, Clinton, was on his way to Newport with 5,000 fresh troops. Sullivan pulled most of his men back to the north end of the island to await D'Estaing's return, leaving only a small force facing the British around Newport.

But as Clinton drew nearer, D'Estaing still hadn't arrived. Following Sullivan's orders, the Americans troops near the front lines pitched their tents, then crept away at two o'clock in the morning, leaving the empty camp to confuse the British. As they pulled back, the Americans laid ambushes along the main East and West Roads. Then they joined the rest of the troops at the north end of the island.

American forces carried this flag during the Battle of Rhode Island. (Rhode Island Historical Society: RHi X4 27)

15

THE BATTLE OF RHODE ISLAND

1 British defensive lines, August 14-28

2 American lines, August 14-28

3 American defensive line, August 29

4 American headquarters

5 Americans ambush Hessian advance, morning, August 29

6 Americans ambush British advance, morning, August 29

7 Hessian Hole, furthest Hessian advance, afternoon, August 29

8 Furthest British advance, afternoon, August 29

9 American retreat by boat, August 30

At daybreak, a long drum roll called the troops together. The Black Regiment was ordered south about a mile. They took cover behind stone walls at the foot of a hill.

Back in Newport, the British realized the Americans were gone when they got no answer to their cannon fire. They marched out after Sullivan's army, hoping to cut off its retreat and destroy it.

Hessian Troops marched up the West Road. These were professional German soldiers hired by the British. The Hessians tried to surround the American troops posted on the hill above the Black Regiment, but the Americans were warned just in time. The Black Regiment covered the retreating American force, firing at the Hessians from a grove of trees.

Then the Black Regiment fell back. They regrouped behind a redoubt: a small, temporary earthen fort with a bristling fence of sharpened poles.

It was a blistering hot day. The men were thirsty and tired. Four British ships sailed up the bay west of them. The ground shook as the British fired their cannons. But the balls fell short. With answering fire, the Americans drove the ships off.

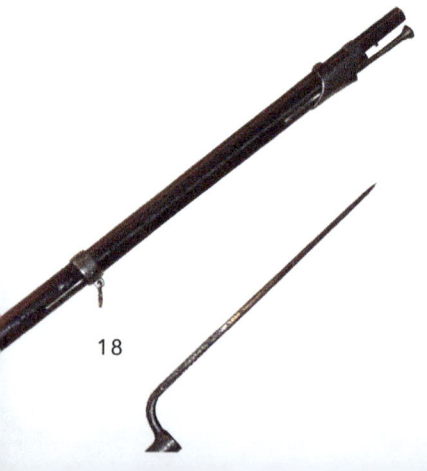

Meanwhile, the Hessians crossed the stream below the Black Regiment. They reformed their ranks in the swampy valley. The crack Hessian fighters expected to punch through the American line where the inexperienced Black Regiment was stationed. The Hessians charged up the hill, wrote one German soldier, toward "wild looking men in their shirtsleeves, among them, many Negroes."

A white American soldier fighting with the Black Regiment described the battle. "Balls, like hail, were flying all around, the man standing next to me was shot by my side." The Hessians attacked twice. Twice the Black Regiment repelled them.

Wiping the sweat from their faces, the men sagged with weariness. Soldiers nearby were sent to reinforce them. As they peered through the

acrid gun smoke, "(the Hessians) attacked us the third time, with the most desperate courage and resolution, but a third time were repulsed."

"Then," General Sullivan reported, "the enemy fled … leaving his dead and wounded." After the battle, thirty Hessians were buried nearby in a hollow that was later named "Hessian Hole." The Hessian leader asked for a transfer, afraid that his men would never follow him into another battle after such heavy losses. A white soldier summed up the action of the day: "Three times in succession, were (the men of the Black Regiment) attacked, with most desperate valor and fury, by well disciplined and veteran troops, and three times did they successfully repel the assault, and thus preserve our army from capture."

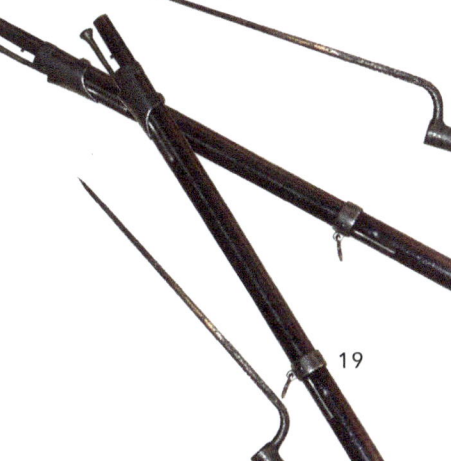

The next evening, the Americans ferried to safety at Fort Barton, on the mainland. They arrived just hours before five thousand fresh enemy troops landed in Newport harbor. General Sullivan boasted that "not a man was left behind, nor smallest article lost."

Two of the Black Regiment had died in the battle. Many more were wounded. Sullivan said the Black Regiment was "entitled to a proper share of the day's honors." One of Washington's most trusted generals called the Battle of Rhode Island "the best-fought action of the war."

After the battle, the Black Regiment stayed in Rhode Island to guard its shores from British raids. The following winter, the war moved south. The British no longer needed Newport, so in 1779 they abandoned it, heading for New York City.

The Black Regiment, along with five thousand French troops, was sent to occupy Newport. It was a particularly harsh winter. So much of Rhode Island had been destroyed during the British occupation that the state did not have enough money to outfit its troops. Soldiers scrounged whatever clothes and food they could find. One French soldier described a black soldier "wearing a cast-off French waistcoat with long sleeves and red cuffs, and a waved helmet with bluish plumes."

In January, 1780, the Black Regiment finally received much-needed supplies and new uniforms. But life was hard and discipline was harsh. Accused of stealing money, sugar, and a silver watch, Cato Brown was given two hundred lashes.

Almost every eighteenth century military unit had its own uniform. A member of the Black Regiment is shown among representatives of other American units at the Battle of Yorktown, Virginia.

BLACKS IN THE REVOLUTION

Of the 300,000 men who fought for the Americans in the Revolutionary War, 5,000 were black. About 10,000 blacks fought for the British. Most of them were Southern slaves. The British promised freedom to slaves who fought for them, but only if their owners were American rebels. Slaves who were owned by men loyal to the British were not offered their freedom.

The next year, the Black Regiment united with the 2nd Rhode Island Regiment to create one racially mixed unit of about 450 men. Colonel Christopher Greene commanded the new 1st Rhode Island Regiment. It joined Washington's troops in New York State. To the south, the British occupied New York City.

The black soldiers from Rhode Island met others like themselves in New York. There were many black men in Washington's army. There were also black troops fighting with the British against them.

The men of the Rhode Island Regiment quickly put up huts. They nicknamed them "Rhode Island Village." Colonel Greene made his headquarters in a house nearby. From this base, the regiment sallied out to raid British troops.

That spring, the Rhode Island Regiment attacked a group of Americans loyal to the British, Delancey's Tories. A few days later, Delancey's men retaliated. Over 200 of them attacked Colonel Greene's headquarters. Only twenty to thirty men were there to defend it, many from the Black Regiment. They were all killed or captured and Greene was killed. It was later said that "the sabers of the enemy only reached him through the bodies of his faithful guard of Blacks, who hovered over him to protect him and every one of whom was killed."

Lieutenant Colonel Jeremiah Olney took command, and the force became known as Olney's Regiment. That summer, French troops joined them and the rest of Washington's troops. The combined armies trained together on the banks of the Hudson River before marching south for what would be the turning point of the war.

The Rhode Islanders were among the first soldiers called to Yorktown, Virginia. By this time they were hardened troops, with a reputation for bravery in battle. They marched south, dressed in linen hunting shirts and overalls. A French marquis wrote in his journal, "At the ferry crossing I met with a detachment of the Rhode Island Regiment. The majority of the enlisted men are Negroes or Mulattoes; but they are strong, robust men, and those I saw made very good appearance." Baron von Closen, second in command of the French troops, said they were merry, confident, and "cheerful under difficulties."

The British troops had been cornered in Yorktown. The allies surrounded them—the French fleet at sea, and combined French and American troops on land. For two months the allies tightened the noose around the British, forcing them back into a smaller and smaller circle.

Two British redoubts blocked the final trench needed to complete the siege. American troops, including the Rhode Island Regiment, were ordered to take the British redoubt on the right, while the French were to take the one on the left. General Washington spoke to the troops, urging them to act the part of firm and brave soldiers. Captain Stephen Olney, who was a relative of Jeremiah Olney and also fought at Yorktown, later said, "I thought then, that (Washington's) knees rather shook, but I have since doubted whether it was not mine."

Captain Olney described the night attack: "The column marched in silence, with guns unloaded and in good order. Many, no doubt, thinking that

less than one quarter of a mile would finish the journey of life with them …
then the enemy fired a full body of musketry." "Huzzah!" shouted the men.
Under British fire, they broke through a fence of sharpened poles. The British
bayoneted Captain Olney, wounding him badly, but his troops poured in
after him. Finally the British gave way, surrendering the redoubt.

The Black Regiment suffered casualties. Bristol Rhodes lost a leg
and an arm. London Slocum was killed. But British losses were much higher,
and the capture of the redoubts sealed their fate.

On October 19, the British surrendered. General Washington and the
French commander sat astride their horses as the British soldiers marched out
of Yorktown. In the celebrations that followed, the Continental Army passed
in review. Baron von Closen declared that the Black Regiment of Rhode
Island was the best American unit, "the most neatly dressed, the best under
arms, and the most precise in its movements."

Yorktown was the last major battle in the Revolutionary War, but the
peace treaty between Britain and the United States wouldn't be signed for
two more years, and the suffering of the Black Regiment wasn't over. They
marched north in the bitter cold. That winter, Plato McClellan lost his toes to
frostbite, and Prince Angell and Cato Brown died. So did 53 other men from
Jeremiah Olney's Rhode Island Regiment.

Hungry and ragged, the remaining men camped out in rough-hewn
huts in Saratoga, New York, awaiting the end of the war.

A young mulatto, Lemuel Hayes, wrote this poem to honor the fallen black patriots of the Revolution.

For liberty, each freeman strives

as it a gift of God

and for it ifield their lives

much better there in death confind

than surviving as a slave.

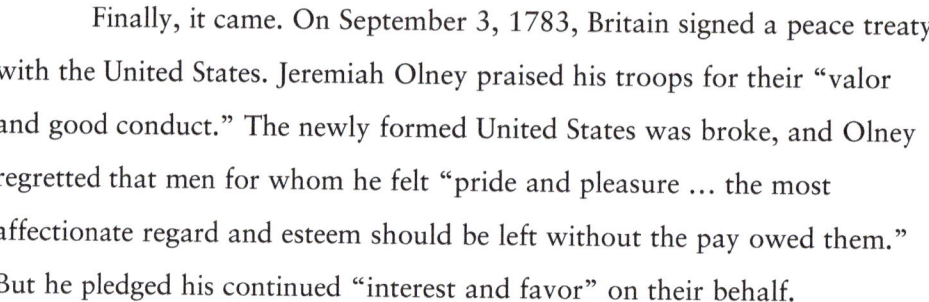

Finally, it came. On September 3, 1783, Britain signed a peace treaty with the United States. Jeremiah Olney praised his troops for their "valor and good conduct." The newly formed United States was broke, and Olney regretted that men for whom he felt "pride and pleasure ... the most affectionate regard and esteem should be left without the pay owed them." But he pledged his continued "interest and favor" on their behalf.

Olney dismissed the brave men of the Black Regiment. Like all foot soldiers of the Revolutionary War, both white and black, they walked all the way home.

What happened when they returned—these men who had fought so hard to earn their freedom? Ebenezer Sisco bought a forty-acre farm south of Providence. Richard Cozzens married a free black woman and had two sons. But most faced struggles of a new sort.

[Handwritten letter, dated Providence 2nd April 1794, addressed to Oliver Wolcott Esq., Comptroller of the Treasury, signed Jere. Olney]

The men of the Black Regiment were free, but most of their families were not. Men worked for years to buy the freedom of their wives and children. Jobs were scarce, and few white people were willing to hire black men. Most ended up doing backbreaking work for very little pay.

Henry Tabor tended a rich man's garden in exchange for half the crop. Bristol Rhodes, who had lost a leg and an arm at Yorktown, worked in a foundry. Brittain Saltonstall went to sea. Many built roads and bridges.

Few received the money the United States owed them. Philip Rodman only received $26—a mere three months' pension—for his service to his country.

Their former commander, Jeremiah Olney, did what he could to help his loyal troops. He wrote to the government, asking for the army pensions due them. He gave them safe passage certificates when they went to sea, and he fought attempts to re-enslave them.

But change was coming. The Revolutionary War tranformed the people who lived through it. As one soldier who had fought beside the Black Regiment said, "Liberty, independence, freedom, were in every man's mouth. They were the sounds at which they rallied, and under which they fought and bled. The word slavery then filled their hearts with horror. They fought because they would not be slaves." How could men who fought for freedom accept the enslavement of others?

Rhode Island Quakers voted that no member of their religion could keep slaves, and they fought to end slavery in the new state. Others spoke out against slavery, too. They pointed to the Black Regiment as an example of the honor and bravery of black men.

A year after the Revolutionary War ended, Rhode Island passed a law that gradually abolished slavery. "Whereas, all men are entitled to life, liberty, and the pursuit of happiness, and the holding mankind in a state of slavery ... is repugnant to this principle ... no person whether Negroes, mulattoes, or others, who shall be born within the limits of this state on or after the first day of March, A.D. 1784 shall be ... slaves."

The process of emancipation took years, because slaves born before the March 1 deadline could be kept in slavery. Children born to slave mothers after that date would stay with their mothers through childhood. But when male children turned twenty-one, and female children turned eighteen, they would be free. Connecticut passed a similar law. Massachusetts and New Hampshire adopted anti-slavery statements into their constitutions.

The last slave in Rhode Island died in 1859. Slavery in New England was coming to an end. On January 1, 1863, President Lincoln struck the deathblow to slavery in the United States with the Emancipation Proclamation.

The bravery of the Black Regiment helped forge the way to freedom. Philip Rodman and Jack Champlin, Henry Tabor and London Slocum, Prince Angell and Bristol Rhodes, and all the men of the Black Regiment fought for liberty and justice for all. Their shining example proved that all men deserve to be free.

1 Valley Forge, Pennsylvania; winter 1777-78; Birth of the plan to enlist slaves for a new Rhode Island regiment

2 Providence, Rhode Island; February 23, 1778; Law passed to create the "Black Regiment"

3 Tiverton, Rhode Island; July 1778; Troops muster at Fort Barton

4 Newport and Portsmouth, Rhode Island; August 1778; Battle of Rhode Island

5 Newport; fall 1779; British pull out, Black Regiment moves in

6 Croton-on-Hudson, New York; spring 1781; Black Regiment in "Rhode Island Village"

7 Yorktown, Virginia; October 19, 1781; the Battle of Yorktown ends

8 Saratoga, New York; 1782-1783; 1st Rhode Island Regiment awaits the end of the war

9 Providence; February, 1784; Rhode Island takes first steps to end slavery, passing a law making children born to slaves free

29

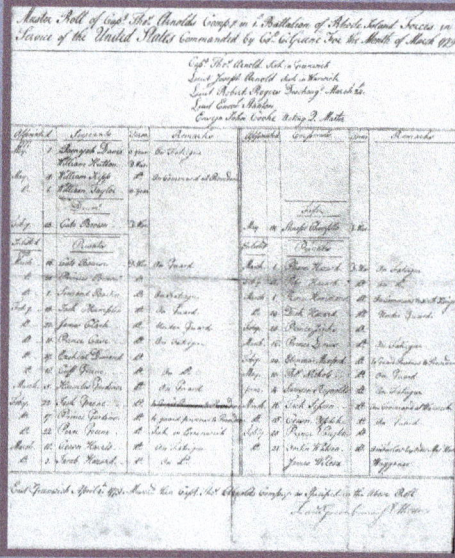

The names of Cato Brown, Jack Champlin, and other black soldiers of the 1st Rhode Island Regiment appear on this 1779 muster roll. (Rhode Island Historical Society: RHi X3 7460)

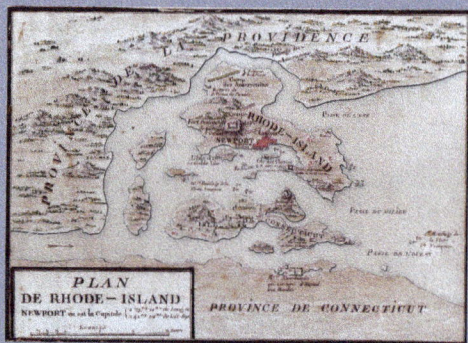

This contemporary French map of the Battle of Rhode Island is both interesting and inaccurate. North is at the left side (not a mistake). The "Rhode Island" in the map is an old name for Aquidneck Island, on which Newport is located. But "Isle de Connecticut' is actually Conanicut Island, and the "Province de Connecticut" isn't Connecticut at all—it's the western part of the state (or colony) of Rhode Island. (Rhode Island Historical Society: RHi X4 28)

GLOSSARY

bayonet:
a knife that fits on the end of a musket, used in close fighting

Continental Army:
the army of the combined states under the leadership of George Washington

emancipation:
the act of freeing someone from slavery

flagship:
the ship carrying the admiral in command of a fleet

militia:
the citizen army of a colony or state

mulatto:
a person of mixed black and white races

musket:
a shoulder gun used by most soldiers in the Revolutionary War

Hessians:
German soldiers paid by the British to fight in the Revolutionary War

pension:
money paid to someone after they retire

privateer:
a privately-owned ship, which is authorized by a government to attack and capture enemy vessels; also, an officer or crew member of a privateering ship

redoubt:
a small, temporary fort, often made of earth with a bristling fence of sharpened poles

regiment:
a military unit of a few hundred soldiers, made up of at least two smaller groups called battalions

safe passage certificates:
papers given to American seamen to protect them from being forced to serve on foreign ships

scurvy:
a disease caused by a lack of vitamin C, causing loss of energy, bleeding gums and other symptoms

TO FIND OUT MORE

BOOKS

Burgan, Michael. *The Untold Story of the Black Regiment: Fighting in the Revolutionary War,* North Mankato, M: Compass Point Books, 2015.

Cox, Clinton. *Come All You Brave Soldiers: Blacks in the Revolutionary War.* New York: Scholastic, 1999.

Martin, Joseph Plum. *Yankee Doodle Boy: A Young Soldier's Adventures in the American Revolution Told by Himself.* New York: William R. Scott Inc., 1964 (based on the narrative published in 1830).

Woelfle, Gretchen. *Answering the Cry for Freedom: stories of African Americans and the American Revolution,* Honesdale, PA: Calkins Creek, an imprint of Highlights, 2016.

WEBSITES

Davis, Robert Scott. "Black Soldiers of Liberty," The Battle of Rhode Island Association, https://battleofrhodeisland.org/black-soldiers-of-liberty/

Geake, Robert A. "In League with Liberty: The Persistence of Patriots of Color and the Formation of the First Rhode Island Regiment of the Continental Army" https://www.americanrevolutioninstitute.org/video/in-league-with-liberty-the-persistence-of-patriots-of-color-and-the-formation-of-the-first-rhode-island-regiment-of-the-continental-army/

Selig, Robert A. "Black Soldiers in the Revolutionary War," https://www.americanrevolution.org/black-soldiers/

PLACES TO VISIT

FORT BARTON, Highland Road, Tiverton, RI: American troops gathered at this site before the Battle of Rhode Island and retreated here after the battle. https://ports-mouthhistorynotes.com/tag/fort-barton/

PATRIOT PARK, junction of Routes 114 and 24 in Portsmouth, RI: Monument to the Black Regiment; site of the stand of the 1st Rhode Island Regiment against Hessian troops during the Battle of Rhode Island.

SARATOGA NATIONAL HISTORICAL PARK, Stillwater, NY: Site of the first major American victory during the American Revolution. The Black Regiment waited out the end of the war here after the Battle of Yorktown. www.nps.gov/sara/

SMITH'S CASTLE, Wickford, RI: historic Rhode Island plantation house where some members of the Black Regiment worked as slaves prior to the American Revolution. www.smithscastle.org/

VALLEY FORGE NATIONAL HISTORICAL PARK, Valley Forge, PA: Site of the winter encampment of Washington's troops where General James Varnum first got the idea of forming the Black Regiment. www.nps.gov/vafo/

YORKTOWN BATTLEFIELD COLONIAL NATIONAL HISTORICAL PARK, Yorktown, VA: site of the last major battle of the American Revolution. The Black Regiment fought here. www.nps.gov/yonb/

INDEX

Angell, Prince, 25

Bayonets, 7
Black Regiment
    Battle of Rhode Island, 15–21
    Battle of Yorktown, 24–25
    combined with 2nd Rhode
        Island Regiment, 22
    created, 3–5
    freed, 26–27
Black soldiers, in war, 22
British soldiers, at
    Newport, 8–10, 13–21
Brown, Cato, 21, 25
Brown, Joseph, 5

Champlin, Jack, 5, 15
Clinton, Gen., 15
Cozzens, Richard, 5, 26

Delancey's Tories, 22
D'Estaing, Count, 10, 13–15

Emancipation, 29

Fort Barton, 8–9, 21
French Navy, 10–14, 15

Gardner, Cuff, 5
Gideon, Harry, 5
Greene, Col. Christopher, 3, 7, 22

Hayes, Lemuel, 26
Hazard, Pharoh, 5
Hazzard, Peter, 13
Hessian soldiers, 16, 18–19

Jenks, Prince, 5

King Philip's War, 4

McClellan, Plato, 25
Mulattoes, 7
Muskets/Musketry, 7

Native American slaves, 4
Newport, RI, 3, 8–10, 13–21

Olney, Capt. Stephen, 3, 24–25
Olney, Lt. Col. Jeremiah, 22, 26, 27

Polock, Asher, 5
Pomp, Jehue, 13

Quakers, Rhode Island, 3, 29

Revolutionary War
    Battle of Rhode Island, 13–21
    Battle of Yorktown, 24–25
    peace treaty signed, 26
Rhodes, Bristol, 25, 27
Roberts, Cuff, 13
Rodman, Philip, 27

Saltonstall, Brittain, 27
2nd Rhode Island Regiment, 3, 22
Sisco, Ebenezer, 26
Slaves/Slavery, 3–5, 29
Slocum, London, 25
Sullivan, Gen. John, 8–9, 10,
    13–15, 19, 21

Tabor, Henry, 5, 15, 27

Updike, Caesar, 5

Varnum, Cato, 5
Varnum, Gen. James, 3
Von Closen, Baron, 24, 25

Washington, Gen. George, 24, 25

ACKNOWLEDGMENTS

Many individuals and organizations contributed to this work, and the author, the illustrator, and the publisher wish to thank most sincerely: Nancy Augustowski, Ann Barrow, the Story Spinners, Barbara Carey, David Clarke, David Cunningham, Frank Daly, Scott Donahue, Kim Hammann, Peter Harrington, Kirk Hindman, Kenneth Giella, Nancy Fairweather Goncalves, Eleanor Keys, Alexander McBurney, Roy Najecki, George Neumann, The Rhode Island Black Heritage Society, The Rhode Island Historical Society, Marshall Sloat, Joaquina Bela Teixeira, Ron Toelk, and Joe Brennan. Special thanks to Captain Richard Sheryka of the Kentish Guards and Captain Carl Becker of the 2nd Rhode Island Regiment for their valuable and generous assistance. All of these individuals and organizations provided information and support and helped correct many errors and clarify historical facts. The editor and the author take full responsibility for any errors that remain.

DEDICATIONS

I dedicate this book to my parents, Vigilio and Nancy Crotta, and to my ancestors who immigrated to this country in search of freedom and justice. L.C.B.

To David, with love. C.K.N.

Library of Congress Cataloging-in-Publication Data
Brennan, Linda Crotta.
The Black Regiment of the American Revolution / by Linda Crotta Brennan;
illustrated by Cheryl Kirk Noll.
p. cm.
Includes bibliographical references (p.) and index.
ISBN-979-8-218-71484-0 (lib. bdg. : alk. paper)
1. United States--History--Revolution, 1775-1783--Participation, African American--Juvenile literature. 2. Rhode Island--History--Revolution, 1775-1783--Participation, African American--Juvenile literature. 3. United States. Continental Army. Rhode Island Regiment, 1st--Juvenile literature. 4. African American soldiers--Rhode Island--History--18th century--Juvenile literature. I. Noll, Cheryl Kirk, ill. II. Title.

Thymely Press are available in bulk for promotional use. Contact the publisher for details Thymelypress@gmail.com.

This reprint was made possible by a grant from RI Society of the Sons of the Revolution.

Printed in USA
Ingram Sparks

Maps by Ron Toelke

Book design by Geraldine Millham

Reprint design assistance by Lisa Greenleaf
www.Lisagreenleafdesign.com